RANDOM MUSINGS.

ONCE UPON A.....STORIES

NEHA SINHA

To the random people who unknowingly inspired me, the nosy
neighbors who gave me stories, the train tracks that carried my
memories, and the endless cups of tea that fueled my thoughts.
To my little one, whose questions made me pause and wonder, and
to the old songs on the radio that made the words flow.
And finally, to lazy lamhe and main aur meri tanhai
moments—thank you for being the quiet magic behind these
musings. This book is as random as life, and all the more special
because of it!

Contents

Foreword — vii

1. Teachers Day — 1
2. ME TOO..... — 4
3. When The Whole World Went Under Renovation — 6
4. This Diwali, Lets…. — 10
5. Its Been A While... — 13
6. Sunsets.... - July 06, 2020 — 16
7. Timelines…. — 19
8. Perspective….. — 22
9. Yesterday, Once More… — 25
10. The World We Live In — 28
11. Pollution….. — 31
12. Vacc"scene" Or Vaccine — 33
13. Shore Amidst The Shor! — 37
14. *Doodh Bhaat* — 40
15. Talc Of The Town: A Powderful Memory! — 44
16. A Steaming Resolution! — 47
17. The Age Cage!! — 50
18. The E-commerce Of Life. — 52
19. Temporary: The Relatable Paradox We Love To Hate — 54
20. The OTT Of Being Overcharged! — 57
21. Main Aur Meri Tanhai Moment ;) — 60
22. The 'lost' & 'Found' — 63
23. The Pride, The Passion, The Game! — 66
24. God Believing: A New Vocabulary For Faith — 68
25. Of Tea, Paranthas, And The Resolution To Pause — 71

Contents

26. From Bow And Arrows To TV Shows   74

27. From "Hamri Atariya Pe Aaja Re" To Swipe Right!   78

28. Living In A Sitcom: Who Are You In Everyone's Story?   82

29. The Swing   85

30. Love At First Insight!   88

31. Zindagi Ka Ganit   92

32. Tick Mark   95

33. Push Or Pull   100

34. Every #Pillow Has A Story!   105

35. Scribbles, Tweets, And Heartbeats: The Journey Of #Words   108

36. Weather Or Whether…..   111

37. 50 Shades Of Grey!   114

38. Mice. Mountains. Mindset.   116

39. The Little Red Man.   118

40. Friday Feels & Table Tales   120

41. Dear December   122

42. Tag Vs.Tug!   124

43. Chhook-Chook Gaadi   126

44. Sunshine Shoes!   130

Foreword

This book is a collection of moments—some fleeting, some lingering, but all of them close to my heart. It's not about life's big, bold chapters but the quiet spaces in between: the lazy afternoons when time seems to stretch, the train tracks that take me back to my childhood, and the strangers who, without knowing it, gave me reasons to write.

These are my musings from random days—thoughts scribbled over tea, memories stirred by old songs on the radio, and reflections sparked by my little one's endless questions. They are not grand or profound; they're just pieces of life, raw and unfiltered, as I've lived and felt them.

If you've ever stopped to savor the smell of rain, been amused by a nosy neighbor, or found joy in a simple memory, you might just find a little bit of yourself in these pages too.

This book isn't meant to preach or teach—it's just my way of pausing to celebrate the beautifully ordinary moments that make up the story of life.

I hope you enjoy this journey through my world as much as I enjoyed writing it.

1
Teachers Day

What do you want to be when you grow up?..... Doctor, army, nurse, pilot, teacher....... !! "A housewife!"came a voice from one distant corner of the classroom. That was a 5 year old speaking her heart n mind. That 5 year old was me.

The teacher told my parents in the ptm about how funny and cute she found that about me.

Dear teacher - "I thankyou for not being judgemental when I expressed what I felt."

I wasn't tagged as the non ambitious child. Nor were my parents made to feel that something was wrong with me.

Things have changed drastically. The classrooms more interactive, teaching is more informative.... the neighbourhoods n friends circle more competitive.... The new generation less sensitive!

That 5 year old child wanted to be a housewife maybe because she heard the word in the house, or maybe cos she looked up to her mother and wanted to be like her, or could be because she found that term really fancy! But it was all cool !

If that exercise is repeated today, my answer would obviously be different. But if someone asked me what would I not want to be? I would not want to be a lot of things....

*A helicopter parent which I often become but then back off! - I'm working on it

The nosy aunty who never minds her own business n often asks my child why she doesn't have the habit of wishing good morning? I know that my child needs to learn and she will ! Please do not lead her to believe that it's an offence.

*The teacher who the children fret - you define the word "school" for them. - Please let there be fondness & eagerness to go to school each morning.

*The boss who takes his title too seriously and gets kicks out of sadistic pleasures - Remember, karma never forgets an address.

*Those who are constantly motivating couples to "start" a family or "complete" the family. - Family is family whether it's just the 2 of us or 3 or 4. We know what we want and we are sure

The dogs that scare the living day Lights out of me! - (who wants to be a dog anyway!!)

And a lot many other things. Let's keep that for another time.

So, what I mean is that, in life, situations , experiences, role models, prominent personalities, people/friends around you teach you a lot. Teach you what you should be like and more of what of who you wouldn't want to be!

When my 6 year old tells me that "When I become prime minister mumma, I would fix these roads

Or "If I was God, I would not make bad words like stupid, silly, kill in this world". It speaks a lot about what and who she doesn't wanna be. She often tells me what I, as a mother should be like - I'm taking notes

To everyone out there who teaches us something everyday - parents, teachers, leaders, friends and family. These tiny eyes - the brigade that we expect will change the world are watching us closely.

They will soon outgrow Spiderman, powerpuff girls, pj masks and the likes....& aspire to be someone who's real. Someone who is "flesh and blood" !

Let's please make an effort to be the force behind " Main badi hoke aapke jaise banna chahti hoon"
Happy teachers day, everyone!
Learn and let learn

2

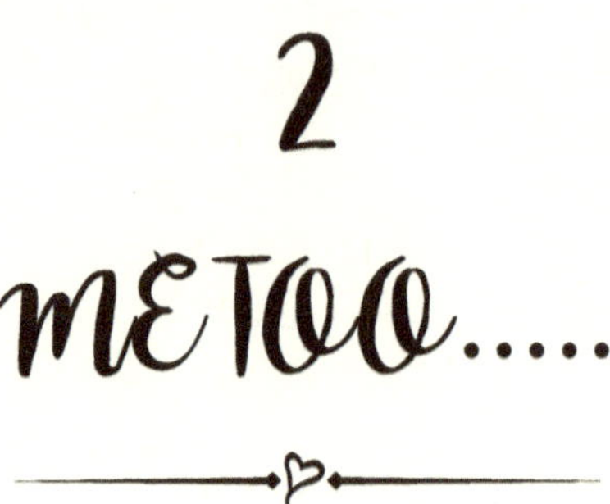

METOO.....

While the "Me too" movement is out there bringing so much charcha on all mediums. I have a different version of the "metoo"!!

I thought of my "metoo" moments too, though mine are solely to do with me , motherhood and my day to day emotions!

So, I let go of my "me too have some ambitions" wala emotion 7 years back and that makes me a full time momma! A mom who willingly quit her job after my daughter was born and I have been very happy in that space so far, touchwood!

And that makes me a mom in the middle. A mom who would like to work yet be home for my kid when she's back from school. And that's the reason I'm still trying to figure out way fwd

But afterall, I'm human too. So yes, when I see other moms goin to work or travelling for work... I have my "kaaaash" me too moment of "getting back to office".

When I open my wardrobe, those formal shirts, blazers are all shouting from their hangers "me too" " me too" ! Thats another "kab pehnungi" metoo.

When I see people go on an all girls trip... I have a doubtful metoo? moment.

I would love to go but I also know that the minute i would land there i will start missing my family! So thats another " confused" me too

When I talk to my ex colleagues and we discuss workplace with some gossip thrown in, I have my "uuufff.. those days..." metoo mode.

When I see some hyper parents hovering around their kids...or pressurising their children for things that aren't necessary... I have a selfdoubting "me too??". Am I also like them? Hope not.

While there is no right or wrong of parenting.. it's To each, his own, but then you do make your own notes of what kind of a parent you wanna be!

When I see kids winning medals and accolades for.something that they have done. The "someday" metoo in me suddenly wakes up!

No. It's not comparison... I would name it as a desire. A desire to see my child also perform and achieve (at her own pace). This feeling is always present in every parent/human. The idea is to nurture it positively instead of getting competitive and worked up about it.

When I see fitness freaks who follow the fitness regime with so much dedication and willpower... I have a metoo feeling with a bit of embarrassment thrown in - me too will start exercising regularly... and then the paranthas and donuts take over. (straight face)

When you see all those lovely faces on screen advertising about the age defying and wrinkle vanishing creams... I make note of which cream to buy next. That's a decision making "metoo" ....!

And many more such instances.....

So the point is that it's ok to have your "metoo" moments of desires, dreams and more.... and to feel what you feeling.. ! The idea is to embrace those moments instead of shoooing them away from your head or feeling guilty & ashamed about them and do what makes you happy :))

And now that I sit n think, it all started with Mohd rafi singing the evergreen "metoo" song -"hum bhi" agar bachchey hotey....naam hamara hota....

3

When the whole world went under Renovation

I believe in zodiac signs.

I've grown up reading a lot of Linda Goodman. So much so that, if any of us didn't get along in the group, we would blame it on our zodiac signs. It was also so much fun to quickly find out zodaic compatibility of our crushes followed by the game of "flakes" and " flames"! Haha... Innocent and cute :)

My zodiac sign is Pisces. As per the book, Pisceans are born dreamers. They see the world through their rose tinted glasses & love to dream and that makes me a true Piscean!

I love to day dream. Like right now while I'm sitting and writing this piece, I'm already on a beach sipping Margaritas. So that's how it works with me ;)

When I talk about dreams, there are 3 types of dreams. The first one is to "day dream", like me, who often dreams about herself in the rapid fire round on Koffee with Karan (I love that Talk show.)

Then there are these "dream big" in life type of dreams. Like for eg. I'm not very ambitious but when I was in school, my dream was to be a in the Student Council and that dream did come true when I was elected as the House Prefect. It was very special :)

And then there are all of us who dream when we sleep. Ofcourse I don't remember all my dreams,

but there are days when I'm dreaming about something beautiful and when I wake up, I want to go back to sleep and begin dreaming from where I left because I didn't want it to end. So, I snuggle back in.

I've also experienced that at times, I wake up from my sleep and it takes me a while to realise and tell myself with a sigh of relief that "Thank god it was just a bad dream".

From the past few days, I'm sure many ... Correction: "all" of us must be going to bed wishing, praying & hoping that tomorrow morning we wake up to " It was just a bad dream" and the headlines read :

"The World finally wakes up from its deep slumber" and the radio stations are abuzz with LataJi & Kishore Kumar in a fusion of,

'Mere khwaaabon mein Jo Aaye & Raat Kali ek khwaab mein aayi..aur gale ka haar hui..."

9

4

This Diwali, Lets....

It's the festival of lights! And so much discussion around banning Chinese lights!

Talking about lights and Chinese goods, I'm reminded of a game we played as children, when we had our "Yayy! Light chali gayi" moment - which btw was pretty often!

And that called for all the kids to come out of their houses and play fun games while our parents chatted away !

Apart from the many games we played, one of them was Chinese whisper. A game, where one person would start the chain and whisper something in the next person's ear and that person to the next and so on....

What happened at the end - what actually reached the last person in the group was very different from what was spoken in the first place!

At times, what happens in life is also pretty much the same! Many times, you generally discuss/talk things with people....a general conversation around anything or any person, experiences etc.

But then it changes many ears and what comes out is an entirely different version of what was actually said/ discussed.

In the game, it was funny to hear the final statement from the last person's mouth, but in real life, it can become quite a nuisance causing unwanted confusion/ drifts.

It's funny how some games which we played as kids & found immense happiness in, could turn out to be an entirely different experience in real life. Luckily, in the game, we got to know what was actually said ! Alas! In real life, it's not the same and so the light chali gayi moment could actually turn out into a "fuse udd Gaya" mode!

Although nowadays we have an option of power back up in evolved/developed cities.

But sadly, there are no backups in relationships!

This Diwali, let's learn to refrain from being away from' a chataai/ladi bomb (the one that ignites from one to the other and the next....) and be a rocket instead. Even if someone ignites a spark, just let it go ..... Up in the air and out of your system.

Happy Diwali :)

P.S. Talking about banning Chinese lights ... Let's first start with banning ourselves from being a part of this game in real life :).

Don't blindly believe all that you hear & remember that a listening ear should not be a running mouth.

Disclaimer: Gossiping is fun as long as it doesn't hurt anyone. :) #ilovetogossip

5

Its been a while...

It's been a while since I cribbed about the traffic in the city.

It's been a while since I requested the restaurant manager to move my name up on the "waiting list for a table."

It's been a while since I texted my friend "I'm stuck in a jam"

It's been a while since I cribbed about missing the 1st five minutes of a movie cos the "parking was full."

It's been a while since I left early for the airport to avoid the "rush" at the check in counter.

It's been a while since I did not fret reading the "newspaper headlines."

It's been a while since I asked my little one to "hug" and make up with her friend after a quarrel.

It's been a while since I saw children fighting for their turn on the swings.

It's been a while since the tiny tots played "Ring a Ring a Roses"

It's been a while since the bride and the groom kissed and said "I do"

It's been a while since we desperately waited for "that" long weekend!

It's been a while since Google saw some new search words.

It's been a while since Math is stuck at number "14" & vocabulary at "Quarantine"

It's been a while, Dear God, it's been a while!

It's been a while since we all sang

"Yeh lamhe, yeh pal hum barson yaad karenge.. Yeh mausam chale gaye toh....hum fariyaad karenge."

6

Sunsets.... - July 06, 2020

Sitting in my balcony yday, seeing the sun go down & turning the sky orange with a shade of blue, I wondered about the ppl in that town of Alaska who recently bid farewell to the sun only to meet and greet with it in January 2020! While it was very tough for me to imagine what it would be like, maybe for them life would go on as usual, or maybe not!

Thinking that it's a good general knowledge topic for my 8 year old to know, I told her about it on our drive to school.

Her first question, "Are they sad?"

"I don't think so. They must have experienced it before too.. every year, maybe!", I replied.

Trying to crack a joke about a poem she had learnt, she said, "Then they can't sing that poem, Suraj nikla hua savera for sooooo many days?!"

"It's all in the mind. Life goes on." I replied, not sure if I really practiced what I just preached. On that note, I hugged her at the school gate and did our daily ritual of blowing flying kisses as she walked towards her classroom.

Driving back after dropping her, I pulled the sunguard to stop the glare from the sun hitting my eyes through the windshield. I quietly thanked God for nothing in particular but it was a big thankyou- that typical thankyou with a deep breath. I can't articulate exactly why I felt like doing it!

The sunset or the sunrise is a play of dark and light which makes it a beautiful treat to watch -The transformation! Else it would be so boring to just have the same blue skies (grey in most cities due to pollution) every day!

It's not easy but it would be so much better if we realised and accepted that life is so much like the sunset and the sunrise.

The setting sun gives way to beginnings. That beautifully sums up the fact that, life goes on!

When we travel to hill stations, the sunset and sunrise points are major tourist attractions. I don't remember if I've ever really sat down & seen the whole process. I get restless maybe when the sun is 3 quarters over the horizon & I turn away.

So many times, in life too, I want to skip ahead through the parts that are slow or painful or lonely, and I want the moment to stop when I'm having fun, I'm enjoying, meeting family friends whom I don't wanna ever let go...or freeze at a single moment of achievement.

But, it doesn't work like that & life goes on. That's what makes it beautiful and enjoyable, I guess.

It's time for me to go pick up Veronica from school. I'm sure she has a lot more questions ready about Alaska and the science behind the setting sun! Google... I'm coming to you!

And guess what's gonna be on loop while I drive ? "yeh jeevan hai.... Is Jeevan Ka... Yahi hai. Yahi hai. Yahi hai rang roop...." #lifeisgood

7

Timelines....

I'm pretty much a phone person. Actually, very much a
phone person! Which means, it's difficult for me
to put my phone away for more than 30 minutes!
And so, every night, before going to bed or after putting
my 8 year old to bed, I like to browse Facebook.
I like to see pretty pictures of my friends travelling to
new destinations, hosting a party, running a
marathon, getting married & general happy pictures.
It's nice to know that people are having a good
time .

I also take notes. Notes which include names of resorts/
restaurants/places/destinations to visit after
seeing them on people's timeline. Saves me the research
work. ;)

But lately, I've been missing all this.
Cos I'm trying to quarantine myself from "Social
Media". I refrain myself from surfing FB before going
to

*bed. Because what I see, is not something very pleasant.
I see fear. I see caution. I see advisory. I see
panic &
I see the World on its knees - All Red & Bruised.*

*Talking about the World, reminds me of this game that
V and I play with the big World Map that we
have. We've to close our eyes and we need to put our
index finger on the map and the place where it
lands is the place we need to research about- atleast 5
facts. The exciting part of the game is to know
the famous things of each country/city.*

*I was just wondering that if we play that game today,
the facts for any place on that map would be the
same. Fear. Panic. Helplessness. Prayers & Lockdown.*

*Today, as I wash my hands for the nth time & light the
camphor dia, I wish and pray for all our timelines
(read: life) to be back with smiles, celebrations, victory
and laughter. May all our faces be back with
smiles instead of masks, our lives full of fun instead of
fear !*

*So that, many like me have a good night's sleep
dreaming about all those beaches where we're making
our sand castles , the hills where we want to go for a
stroll, the parks bustling with giggles et all.*

*And while I write this article, I'm reminded of Juhi
Chawla fearlessly singing "Dilli se gayi Poona... Poona
se gayi Patna...."*

*May we all have that spring in our step very soon &
always!*

#vanishcoronavirus   *#safetravel*   *#world*
#healthiswealth

8

Perspective......

So, it's officially monsoon season in Bangalore. You wake up to cold and cloudy mornings, so breezy that the first thing you do is wear a jacket after you step out of the bed.

In a normal situation, I would be happy about the cloudy weather being romantic etc but nowadays the homemaker in me takes over the romantic in me and my first thought is "how will the clothes dry?" And the paranoid me screams, " thanda mausam...let's keep warm" Anyways, let's keep this discussion for another day, another write up!

So about last evening! I was making rotis for dinner listening to some good old songs. Listening to songs while I do my kitchen work makes it easy for me cos then the mind wanders elsewhere and I don't really " crib" about all the work that I have to do given that house helps are not around. Ofcourse the genre of songs depends on the mood that I'm in ! And so, yesterday it was "romantic". Thanks to the weather!

Whoever knows me well would be aware how much I "hate" cooking! And that obviously explains the extent to which I miss my cook whenever I'm in the kitchen.(I'm sure many of u do). Then I tell myself, jab cook aayegi tab yeh banwaaungi, Woh karaaungi etc. Lekin woh tab aayega kab?!

And just when I was engrossed in all these thoughts, the line in the background song made me smile, " Aaj phir Dil ne ek tamannaaa ki. Aaj phir Dil ko humne samjhaya"

During BC (Before Corona) days, maybe this song would have just been a song which I would enjoy listening to and humming along. But yesterday, this line caught my attention.

Maybe because something within me is hoping praying and looking forward for a miracle to happen which will take all this chaos in the world away! But, till then we need to wait and "samjhaao" ourselves to keep the faith. Regularly!

Somewhere I needed that reassurance, and tell myself that it's not a question of "if" it's just a question of "when" and it's THIS "when" that we all need to wait out for, even though we are all running out of patience & faith. And for me, that came in through this song & I smiled.

Basically, It's all about the fact that we filter and see things from what we are going thru at "that" moment. On some days, some songs are just pure music and on other days..... Each of the lyrics make so much sense. Like it did to me yesterday.

And guess what? However dramatic it may sound to you. For me, I would call it "God sent" (in disguise: Alexa) specially in these times. The next song that played right after, from the movie QSQT......the lines were " Ab hai judaaai Ka mausam, do pal Ka mehmaan.... Kaise na jaayega andhera. Kyun na thamega tufaaan....."

And this time I giggled to myself..not only because I was happy and filled with hope of meeting family and friends soon but because I thought how conveniently it all makes sense when you want it to!

As someone rightly said, "What we see depends mainly on what we look for"

It's the way you look at things. We see what we want to see and we hear what we like to hear!

#diltohpagalhai#dilkibaat

24

9

Yesterday, once more…

Yesterday, my 8 year old made a video of a cot she had made for her doll. She wanted me to send it on Whatsapp, which I did. What started exactly after 5 minutes of me sending that video is the reason I'm writing this piece.

So, exactly after 5 minutes of sending that video, my mini me comes to me to check, if they've replied? Upon checking, I told her that they haven't. And then her impatience knew no ends. The follow up happened every 5 minutes ! And when then they finally did, I didn't tell her. I told her after a while. What I also did was converted our night bedtime story session into " humaare zamaane mein" tales. Gosh! That makes me feel so old.

Maybe I over analyzed the situation or over reacted. Maybe I was just being a "mom"

But that's not the point. What I realised was that this "instant" world has created a lot of unrest in our lives. Instant messages, instant replies, instant books, instant gifts and the list is long.The only thing I remember that was instant in our times was Maggie which also took 2 minutes to cook!

I still remember writing letters to my friends and family.. decorating them with stickers on a beautiful letter pad and then carefully licking that vertical line on the envelope to seal it. Even though we wrote, sealed with a kiss ..we all knew it was spit all the way...! Okay..in some cases, gum (yeah..that's what we called glue) And then eagerly "waited" for the postman to deliver "my letter". The joy back then was to see the letter addressed to "me" !

Gifts and presents were an annual affair. Eating out was again limited to anniversary and birthdays. Movies would only have songs as their promos which made us yearn for it to release in theatres to find out what the story was. Finding out a word meaning meant referring to The dictionary or Thesaurus. Patiently and systematically going thru the pages alphabetically.

Weekend Outings were visits to uncle auntie houses. And no! No prior calls were made to announce that we are coming. Many a times, we would reach and find a taala at the entrance and then my father would meticulously take out his visiting card and place it at the door saying " haajri toh laga dein". And then we would go to another friend's house. Again, without "appointment". Which often made the moms feel embarrassed when they would find the biscuit and namkeen box empty because the children had eaten them all. Hahah...And many times it would turn into a "khaana yahin kha ke jaana" and we all ate whatever was made or a quick pulao would do the trick! . ....And it was all fun and fine.

No body would mind.

Phone calls in our times were about landlines, blank calls , prank calls and wrong numbers. The race to reach the handset to pick up the phone wasn't less than any Olympic event. Because one didn't know who's calling, that excitement was always there. And we would always pick up the phone because you never know who it could be. Unlike now, where we have the option to hear, see and then mute the call to only answer it later.

In all this, maybe we didn't realise but it was all about thehraav (Hindi word), patience, effort, excitement, yearning, being less judgemental, I don't think back then, we took things for granted. Some may call all this primitive but I'm old school so....

and ofcourse everything has its pros and cons!

What's changed in today's age is the existence of read receipts, double tick, blue ticks, caller id of the world.

You send/get a message and you don't get a reply/reply back to it, God help u. Ofcourse, some people have achieved Nirvana and disabled the blue tick. Live and let live types! But the point is

What have we welcomed in our lives in this process?

Unrest, expectations, assumptions, presumptions, impatience.......

Talking of patience, as they say, Patience is virtue. But given the current pandemic, I'm not sure how much patience from my growing up years, which I just bragged about in the above few...err many lines is coming to use right now! Cos, all that we are "impatiently" waiting for is the vaccine!

Meanwhile, on my playlist "Allah ke bande Hans de ..Jo bhi ho kal phir aayega"

10
The world we live in

My father travelled extensively for work.

Yet there was never a thought of worry in my mumma's world.

No periodic updates of where he has reached.

Not even in case of a train missed!

We saw our cousins once a year.

And when they came visitng, there was so much thrill n cheer!

No phones, no messages, no WhatsApp calls.

Relations back then were still so strong!

No phones or cameras to capture each thing, yet life was never ever Boring!!

School was fun riding our bicycles on the busy roads.

We would go in a group or even alone. And yes, without a cell phone!

Today when I have to send my lil one to the park.

A 10 minute drill of good touch bad touch and strangers is what we talk!

What has life come to!

Gadgets, killings, terror and more.

I am not even getting to innocence being raped behind closed doors.

Today I'm teaching my child not to trust anyone.

At such a tender age when life for her has just begun.

Faith is a word that's gone with the wind.

All thats left is fear and a world thats sinned.

I read the news and my heart begins to sink!

What am I doing... what's all this, I sit and think.

I remember our childhood when it was safe n fun.

What kinda world are we giving to our little ones!

11

Pollution......

In light of current pollution level in the city, my friend and I were fondly remembering old times. Remembering our train journeys with parents, when we carried water in kool kegs! Nobody "sold water then!

Delhi was our pit stop for summer holiday destination every year (on way to my massi's house in bikaner). Out of the Few things that I identified with the capital, one was "machine ka thanda paani" wala bhaiyas standing at bus stops everywhere in the city. I found it very amusing! Why would they sell water, I wondered!

And now we are in the bisleri age! Bottled water as we say. Water is a precious commodity. We pay for Water!

We have seen the transition from drinking water from taps in school to water being sold!

And Today, while Vedica is jumping with joy seeing a fancy device in her room which changes color, my heart aches to think about the fact that "did I just pay to buy some pure air to breathe?"

What have we come to! What are we leaving behind for our kids!?

Yet another year will pass. We will crib, complain, sign petitions, install apps to check the aqi, share videos of mishaps, upload photos and instances and express our anger & concerns on various platforms.... and nothing will change.

What will change is the AQI - from bad to worse to worst!

12

Vacc "scene" or Vaccine

Our school recess was for 30 minutes...sometimes 25 depending on the subject teacher just before the recess. If she decided to take 5 minutes extra to wrap up, we had to hold on our temptation to go out and also our hunger pangs.

Tiffins usually had home cooked food by Mummy except for days (which was probably once or twice a month) when I was given Rs.10 to buy something to eat from the school canteen & that served as lunch for that day! I called it "Canteen Day".

Our school canteen was run by a Gujarati couple whom we called Maasi and Maasa .. They stocked samosas with imli chutney served in newspapers, puff, chocolates and pepsi cola- a frozen cola drink in a long pillow shaped plastic wrapper which was almost chewed on to sip it. (and here I am! A mother who *freaks out if V tries to tear open the wrapper of a chocolate with her teeth! Call me paranoid.*

Okay, so back to the canteen. The canteen was a decent size with a big entrance amidst our sports field. After a few steps from the entrance, there was a rod beyond which we weren't allowed. The other side was where food was made, displayed and served. Tempting.

So, the Canteen days were high pressure days. Somewhat like the fastest finger first. If you just replace the finger with legs... you will get what I'm talking about. If you were in luck on your canteen day, on hearing the recess bell, one would sprint from the classroom to the canteen, skipping 2 stairs at a time and reach there and be amongst the first ones to get your grub.

God forbid, if the subject teacher just before the recess took a few minutes extra to wind up, you had to actually almost fight a war. You entered the canteen with a huge crowd of students, screaming "Maasi, ek samosa aapo, bey puff aapo" (Gujarati) with their hands stretched out in air to the other end of the rod to either pay for their order or receive them. In all that cacophony & chaos, you had to be really lucky if:

1. YOU WERE TALL & HAD LONG ARMS.

2. MAASA MAASI HEARD YOUR VOICE

3. BY THE TIME THEY HEAR YOU, STOCK IS STILL THERE.

If the above 3 conditions were met then one would come out of the crowd victorious although with disheveled hair, crumpled uniforms, stained shoes and a big grin on their faces. Yayy.. ready for the world. Bring it on!

On other days, you would still come out of the crowd with disheveled hair, crumpled uniforms, stained shoes but empty handed!!

Hmph! All the hard work for nothing. After all, you waited for your canteen day! Disappointed.

But then what are friends for ? The tiffins were shared while one still drooled about the samosas thinking, chalo aaj nahi phir kabhi.

There was no system of queues or tokens maybe cos of the time constraint. The younger kids would either ask their elder siblings for help or any of the many didis.... the concept of ek ki didi sabki didi.

As I sit with my phone to book a vaccine for the past few days, I realise that this race is also based on fastest *finger first maybe NOT!*

If you are in luck till the stocks last, you will get the slot!

If not, what are friends for? Rant & Frustrations can be shared and so can hope, info and hacks around it.

Note to self: Keep at it & plug in earphones to :

Kuch Paane Ki Ho Aas Aas
Kuch Armaan Ho Jo Khaas Khaas
Aashaayein ...
Har Koshish Mein Ho Waar Waar

Kare Dariyaon Ko Aar Paar....Aashaayein....

P.S. Just subtly letting out my frustration with a pinch of hope thrown in. :)

Kisi ne.sach hee kaha hai, Ummeed pe duniya kaayam hai.

13

Shore amidst the Shor!

———❤———

Let me share with you an adventurous incident from my trip to Sri Lanka a few years back. We were 8 of us. The trip was spent visiting turtle hatcheries, relaxing on the beach, shopping, hogging on sea food and some " water sports". Yes, it deserves the respect of the inverted commas for a reason & you will soon know why!

So, we arrived at the site for water sports chosen by us after some bit of research and recommendations. 6 of us got onto the bright yellow banana boat and off we went!

This is the only memory I have, of being "on" the banana boat cos the next thing I remember is being thrown into n diving deep down, seeing green dirty water and finding myself afloat in the creek with others floating around me at various distances. The speed boat couldn't be spotted! Guess the driver took the name "speed" boat quite literally!

Now, why the speed boat went so far can be attributed to *Newton's 1st law of motion- I think

Anyways, so when the person on the speed would have realized that we've toppled over, he came back to the point where we were trying to stay afloat with our "so called" life jackets. And out of that, only 3 of us were swimmers, so u can understand the anxiety and panic. This also included an 8 year old. Goose bumps!

Now began the real adventure of getting back on the boat! Any person's first reaction should have been to figure out how to get onto the boat and be safe.

But, because of my fear, anger, frustration I started hurling abuses and shouting at the driver for his irresponsible act of putting our lives in danger! Good sense prevailed and I realized that the need of the hour for all of us is to be back on the boat to be safe! The complains can wait.

So with a push and a pull, a hand here n a hand there, we finally managed to be back on the speed boat which ferried us to the shore. Phew!

Once we were back, we obviously took it up with the service provider!

Lesson learnt: This particular water sport is not the most reliable. Yet if we want to indulge in it, we need to make sure of the service provider we choose by doing our bit of research, but no guarantee! The nature of the sport is such!

To cut a long story short, the whole country is in a lot of mess. We don't want others to tell us how badly who's screwed up. We all know and that's a never ending debate.

The priority for all us right now should be to figure out a way to make it better in any way we can and doing what we can in our capacity.

By sharing resources

by sharing recovery stories

By sharing validated information

By posting a prayer

By following rules

By motivating mental health......... by. ....

We all are feeling frustrated , failed, angered and fearful. But spreading fear and anger on social media platforms is not helping either. It only adds to the anxiety!

Like I mentioned above, the need of the hour is to get back on the boat .by supporting , motivating and helping each other in whichever way we can!

When the time comes, when we reach the shore, we can always make our choices for the next ride. We can always make a more informed decision. It will never be a safe, fool proof ride coz the nature of the sport is such!

But for now,

Saathi haath badhaana.....

*Disclaimer : I'm a commerce student..

14
Doodh Bhaat

Of all the gradual things in this life, watching your kids grow up is perhaps a bag full of mixed feelings. For me, at times, It is difficult and sometimes delightful..... depending on the day, my mood, the state of her room, the weather or maybe just my level of PMS.

Honestly, this past one year has gone by unnoticed in many ways.. a large part of their growing up..we attribute to the class that they go to every year.... we make room for new uniforms.... every school day is different.. the books that they get from the library also gives us a sense that they're growin up.. the Sports day races change from dress up relay to flat races, the tales from their "tete a tete" with friends change...and so on... etc. But none of that happened last year ! And if I can give a term to the year gone by, it would be *doodh bhaat*

*I'm not sure if many of u would have ever heard this term ... this is basically a term we used as.kids ..if there was a child in the group who.was very young to understand the game but still wanted to be a part of it, we would say "uska doodh bhaat hai "which essentially meant that the child wouldn't play the den and would be exempted from penalties etc. basically be a part of the play but " *wont be Counted**

So yes, 2020 was a doodh bhaat year for me as far as my kid is concerned. And why not!

So what, if their shoe size increased from a 34 to 36 or for that matter, the genre of books changed from Aesop fables to mystery & PJ masks (aargh! This is what life has become literally.. in our PJs all day and masks!!) was replaced by Horrid Henry!

A year of not meeting friends and family, of not visitng your favourite book store or not going out to eat "that" dish in your favourite restaurant is nothing but DOODH BHAAT...ie. NOT COUNTED. Bas.

Lately, V's favorite thing to do is to rummage thru my wardrobe and pick up a dress of mine ....make it fit with clips and hair ties around it ....wear my heels and be in that attire for.the whole day...the heels eventually come off cos obviously they aren't comfortable for her and then she comes n stands besides me to see how tall she's grown.... n with a big grin on her face declares that she's reached till my bust.....my shoulder and almost my lips!....all in a week's time (As per her) . I dont correct her either. Instead, I make the most of that opportunity by sliding in a quick comment " See, this is what happens when you eat well and cycle"! Hah... Victory! But honestly, watching them grow is a bitter sweet feeling.

I can't generalise the feeling but I can definitely speak for myself....

To me , it feels like ...... a game of pakda pakdi where your'e chasing but not being able to catch, it feels like cribbing about the mess on certain days while knowing very well that it will all be tidy one day and terribly missed..it feels like a lump in the throat....

And sometimes it also feels like freedom! And this part is hard to accept cos even though I know that she's becoming herself, I'm confused. Afterall, we are all in the midst of our own transitions, our own acceptance, our own becoming.

Even though were all grown up ....we r still growing up....

Meanwhile, somewhere in the world someone must be listening to.... aanewala pal jaane wala hai...... :)

*P.S The above article is a work of pandemic over think.
:)*

43

15
Talc of the Town: A Powderful Memory!

———♡———

Recently our subjects got split into Physics, Chemistry & Biology.

So, obviously, that's a lot of work. Trying our best to make it entertaining and interactive so that boredom doesn't set in and the basics seem simpler.

One such Chemistry discussion led us to talk about Talc. Very proudly my not-so-little one announced the composition – Oxygen, Silicon and Magnesium and waited for me to applaud for the promptness and memory! She also had an abbreviation to remember it better – It's an 'OSM' (read: awesome) powder Mumma - Big 'See, I am so smart' Grin on her face!

And that's the adjective which took us down memory lane! Quite an 'Awesome' powder for sure!

I'm unsure if many children today would really know what talcum powder is. Okay! Maybe they've heard it or seen it in commercials or tv ads. But how many of us still have a bottle of talcum powder at home?

Remember the days, when every dressing table had this towering personality standing tall with its other pals gathered around it – Shilpa Bindi, comb, lipsticks, kajal, body lotions, and ponds cream were the common ones. It was quite a 'fragrant and good-looking family'. The tallest being the head of the family – 'The talcum powder!' My visual memory of the same is a tall soft plastic POND'S bottle with pink and white flowers on it or a red tin bottle with Cinthol written on it.

The dots on the top of the bottle were such a plaything – unclogging them by piercing a toothpick or a safety pin in it – so satisfying and fun! Best way to develop hand-eye coordination – Fine motor skills, you see

Apart from being the head of the clan, it also left quite an ' impression' around. Those armpits when smothered with talcum powder after bath created quite a 'storm' around and below the dressing area that could rival any tropical cyclone! And who could resist the temptation of tracing the alphabet or making drawings on it?

How can we forget the ingenious reuse of these bottles as piggy banks in most houses? A slit at the top of the rotating cap and Viola - they transformed into treasure chests for our tiny fortunes!

Be it a lazy breakfast in bed with a hot cuppa coffee/tea spilling on the bed or prickly heat – Talcum to the rescue! Back then when matte lipsticks were not as famous – we would dab a little powder on the applied lipstick and just press it with a tissue – it was after all a 'MATTE'r of fashion and style!

Oily & Dull face – Just dab a little.

Stinking shoes – Here it comes!

A game of carrom – Sprinkle it!

Quite a multi-talented personality, eh?

Replaced by deodorant sticks, deo sprays, and perfumes, it now exists as a faint memory of a fragrant and good-looking family from the past. Alas!

The talcum powder disappeared into 'thin air' – quite literally!

Farewell, dear talcum powder, you were truly an 'awesome' powder that left an 'impression' on our lives! May your fragrant spirit continue to sprinkle joy and memories in the hearts of those who remember you fondly.

Okay! Back to Chemistry for now!

Mood: Le Gayi Khushboo maang ke bahaar......

16

A Steaming Resolution!

The final countdown to another year! It's that season when we juggle reflections on the year gone by with the enthusiastic planning of the year about to unfold – Resolutions!

If I could put the past year in a nutshell then – it was surely a whirlwind of learning curves, moments of introspection and running to follow and stick to 'schedule.'

Between job commitments, household chores (that seem to multiply like rabbits), being a chauffeur to hobby classes (seriously, I could give competition to an Uber driver!), projects, exams, and the extra-curricular activities that take on a life of their own. Amidst all this, my humble cup of tea transformed from piping hot to lukewarm and breakfast resembled an arctic expedition's remnants.

And when I look back, I realise that amidst all these scheduled marvels, there's a missing link called 'ME-time'. You know where self-grooming isn't a pending task and where I drink my tea while it's actually steaming with enthusiasm just like a 2-year-old's excitement on seeing bubbles being blown in the air!

So, here I am, trying to do the year-end ritual - making a resolution. No, not the clichéd 'hit the gym every day' kind (although kudos to those who conquer that mountain!).

Mine is the "I will rescue my tea from the fate of going lukewarm, eat my paranthas while the butter melts on them, and finally prioritize self-care"! Yes, that also includes applying the 'very expensive' night cream before going to bed instead of letting it sit pretty on my dressing table!

Because it's high time I hit the pause button. It's about turning the 'warm' moments into 'hot' ones and bidding farewell to procrastination.

So, for all those of you out there who like to sip your Tea hot, here's to 2024 filled with piping hot tea/coffee, breakfasts eaten at a leisurely pace, and self-care routines that make us feel like royalty amidst the madness.

May the only thing that's warm in 2024 be: WARM hugs and the WARMTH of relationships!

Current mood: Ek garam chai ki pyaali ho....... Koi usko 'Peene' wali ho!

17

The Age Cage!!

—♥—

We recently moved into a new condo and like any parent, I hoped my daughter would quickly make new friends. But friendships can sometimes be tricky, especially when you're almost a teenager. And to be honest, there's more drama with the girls, while the boys seem to just want to play without all the group dynamics.

So, my daughter has always found herself enjoying more with a mixed-age group of kids. She usually clicks better with kids who are 1-2 years younger, though she does have some great friends her own age at school! Touchwood.

The other day, the older girls noticed her playing with the not-so-old kids and asked, "Why are you hanging out with them? Aren't you almost a teenager?" This confused her. She wanted to fit in with the girls her age, but she was having way more fun with the younger kids. It's like she was stuck between being herself and trying to meet the expectations of being a "big girl." Dilemma.

My daughter's struggle between fitting in with the older girls and having fun with the younger ones made me question whether friendships always 'have' to follow a set path. Shouldn't It be okay to make friends with people who are younger or older if that's where you find happiness? Do we really need to have rules here? Cliche.

It's like going to a buffet but only eating from one section. Sure you might enjoy it, but what if the best dish is on the other side of the table? Friendships aren't and shouldn't always be about age. It should infact be about finding people who make you laugh & smile, who get you, and who make life a little brighter! Whether they're younger, older, or somewhere in between - shouldn't be the deciding factor! Choices.

So, here's to friendships that break the age & the gender cliche, to connections that don't follow the rules, and to raising kids who are brave enough to follow their hearts—even if it means playing superheroes with the little ones while the older kids look on!

18

The E-commerce of Life.

Having so many shopping #apps on my phone means it constantly buzzes with notifications: "Last Chance to Buy!", "Only 1 Left in Stock!", "Hurry, Sale Ending Soon!"—it's like they're personally challenging my willpower. And honestly, sometimes I'm eyeing a dress, thinking, "I'll wait for a bigger discount," only to realize it's suddenly out of stock! Oops.

That got me thinking—life is a lot like online shopping, isn't it?

For example. # WhatsApp. We all have friends who're like #Amazon Prime—responding to messages almost instantly, like they're always "in stock" and ready for next-day delivery. You send a message, and boom, they're there with a reply faster than you can hit send. It's comforting, right?

But then, there's the other type of friends. The ones who reply after hours, or sometimes even days. And by the time they reply, you've either forgotten the context of the conversation or Lost interest in it. It's like ordering something with "Delivery in 5-10 business days," Firstly, you wonder whether to order it or not, then you look for options, and if at all, you end up ordering, and it says arriving late....by the time it arrives, you've practically forgotten you even ordered it. You're left wondering - whether it's useful or not! Might as well just #Returnitem

I'm not tagging them to be good/bad-just stating habits and their effect on us. :)

You know that feeling when you see a notification that there's only "1 left in stock"? Well, I get #FOMO—it's a mix of panic and excitement. #Relationships can feel the same way. It's like when you're casually browsing and think, "I'll come back for it later," only to find it's #soldout. Relationships, just like inventory, can run low if we don't restock it regularly. Don't wait until the "Out of Stock" sign appears—give it time, appreciate the attention, and show your love and appreciation while you can!"

#Work is no different. If you're the go-to person in office, it can feel like you're always in everyone's 'Add to Cart'—ready to solve problems, take on extra tasks, fill in for someone, and save the day! But, just like leaving items in your online cart for too long, people may start assuming you'll always be there, no checkout necessary! Know your Value - Big Note to self.

Just like that last item in stock, anyone's availability isn't guaranteed forever. Don't let anyone take you for granted until you're metaphorically "out of stock."

So, whether it's friends, relationships, family, or work, make sure to appreciate the people and things in your life before you get hit with that dreaded "Out of Stock" sign. Go ahead, click #Add to Cart" and hit #Checkout" with a heartfelt conversation, a quick reply to the #Whatsapp message, or an outing over a cup of coffee or a tequila shot ;)—whatever suits!

Because trust me, just like that perfect dress or that fast reply from a friend, nothing should be #takenForgranted.

After all, we are all "Limited Stock Available," aren't we?

Mood: one of my all time favourites!

Ajeeb daastan hai yeh...

19

Temporary: The Relatable Paradox We Love to Hate

Disclaimer: This is not a preachy post. just some realisations and "note to self". :)

"#Temporary"—a wonderful word that somehow manages to both freak us out and comfort us!

Ofcourse its the mantra and the principle on which #life is based and it's only wise to approach life like that. But as they say, " too much of a good thing is also a bad thing".

Life is full of these fleeting moments. Sometimes, we thank god that somethings are #temporary. Like some unpleasant & painful experiences, the never-ending google meetings, a bad hair day,

;) while other times, we cling to things & wish they werent temporary, like that extra 15 minutes of snoozing, a relationship / friendship or moments spent with someone special- friends & family!

It's all about #context.

But I've come across some ppl who take the phrase "everything is temporary" very seriously. And I feel that in all this, they are missing to FEEL. (debatable!)

While I admire their zen-like detachment, I often wonder—if they approach everything as temporary, then do they really feel what we're supposed to feel?

There is a very thin line between #temporary & #Indifferent. Indifference is "temporary's" much cooler but emotionally unavailable cousin. It shrugs at everything & says "meh" to every experience.

While I myself listen to a lot of Sadhguru & I'm all for the "this too shall pass" pep talk when things get tough. We all need a little #hope to cling to when we're knee-deep into things we cant control, but to be honest: labeling everything as temporary feels like a convenient little emotional loophole. You get to skip over the messiness of feeling too much or getting attached but somewhere you miss out on feeling those precious in-between moments—the good, the bad, and the absolutely hilarious. Won't it come out eventually ? Im suddenly reminded of the programme

" the floor is lava" ;)

#Emotions are supposed to be felt! Surely don't let them consume you but without feeling these emotions, we forget to appreciate things, love fully, live boldly & laugh loudly! We forget to FEEL.

So, Note to self & our future generations: continue to #believe that all storms run out of rain. But sometimes, we are supposed to feel the rain & enjoy jumping in the puddles.

Mood: aane wala pal jaane wala hai...

20
The OTT of Being Overcharged!

Today I got a notification that my subscription for a particular OTT platform has been renewed. Then I realised that I hardly watch that OTT platform and I had subscribed to it for a 'particular' movie which was apparently only on that platform. Aargh. Money wasted.

Sometimes I feel, these notifications should be audio..recorded by Moms of teenagers who can then yell 3 times or probably more to remind us again & again & AGAIN.

Next step: Stop subscription.

Anyways, so the point I was coming to is that it's funny how "paying" "used" to mean something. I pay for Amazon Prime, but I still have to rent some movies.

I've subscribed for Netflix, yet I'll still get ads. I need to subscribe to the premium version of Spotify and YouTube just to avoid ads!

Swiggy, milkbasket, big basket..... all of these!

Back in the day, paying meant we had a deal! I valued the service enough to pay, and the business appreciated that by making sure I didn't regret it. That unspoken contract? Pretty much gone now. Paying doesnt really guarantee better service—it just means the business sees you as someone they can extract more from - whether it's through upsells, ads, or convincing us to provide free content. It's like they've created a business model inside another business model wrapped in yet another business model. Wow! Like a gift wrap. only to be disappointed later.

The more we consume, the less power we have. Consumerism was supposed to be about choice and value, but ..but...but!

Instead of putting in the effort to attract new customers which by the way is very tough, companies seem more focused on milking the ones they've already got for every penny they can.

Yes! Rant post.

Deal with it.

Every post cant be about GYAAAN else Sadhguru will have competition no?

tee hee! ;)

21

Main aur meri tanhai moment ;)

Yesterday evening, I was sitting by the window and having my cup of chai & scrolling through my phone, which was at 5% battery! After a while, it conked off! Too lazy to go get the charger, I sat there looking outside the window, sipping on chai! So,evening chai was just Main aur meri tanhaai - jo aksar kaafi baatein karte hain. :)

The view from the window is of tall buildings—they call it the Mumbai skyline. Then there is the sea link, which plays hide-and-seek depending on the pollution levels—so it's mostly in Hide mode! Yday evening, the sunset was beautiful—I'm sure it is so every day, just that I am too engrossed in scrolling through my phone, either talking/chatting with a friend over the phone, checking mails or watching the sea of influencer videos on social media. Eye roll to self!!

And that makes me wonder that nowadays, every other person on the internet is an influencer. I'm not even sure who actually gets influenced in the first place cos everyone is an influencer! Figure of speech: Hyperbole. The situation is so absurd that even the influencers are influenced by other influencers. It's like a giant, glittering domino effect. But do we really relate to all of them?

Like, some of them have made the morning coffee look sooo glamorous with a photo of themselves and the coffee cup with a caption that says, "woke up looking like this" with a #nofilter hashtag. No sleepy eyes, no dishevelled hair, no toothpaste stains on the night suit, ironed PJs... etc. etc.I mean, it makes me doubt

and question everything at that moment! All my life is a LIE?? Meanwhile, my cup of tea isn't hot anymore. Aarghhhh.

I want to start a trend of "woke up looking like this"—GROGGY, Rubbing eyes, crushed PJs. with the hashtag #relatable. But then, who will be influenced by that, I WONDER? sigh.

Note to self - I think we need a shift.

Instead of scrolling through my phone for SM Content, I want to be busy getting influenced by the REAL & OG Influencers—the rising sun, for instance. No filter needed, no sponsored content—just pure, unadulterated beauty that's been influencing humanity since, well, forever. Why do you think there are Sunset Point and Sunrise Points in tourist spots? Tell. Tell.

Or how about the rain? There's no influencer out there who can compete with the simple pleasure of raindrops or the smell of rain - Petrichor is the word! :)

The thunder? It's like the sky's own personal rock concert with a drum solo that no background score can match! And the lightning? It's the first natural camera with a flashlight & that too without a single filter. :)Smile. Momma Nature is clicking a picture! ;)

or maybe the birds or just the clear skies........!!

Okay, Baby steps. Step 1: When alone, morning and evening tea time will be without a cell phone.Decision taken !

So this morning, for me, started with me sitting and enjoying the aroma of freshly brewed tea, gazing outside the window and watching the flight of parrots (yes, there are surprisingly quite a few in our vicinity! Rare.), and just being!

These moments of pure, unedited life are the true influencers. They shape our moods, our days and our being! They don't need followers or likes to validate their worth. Just a few ppl like you and me! :)

Because, at the end of the day, it's not really about Who's influencing whom? but rather, What's worth being influenced by?

22
The 'lost' & 'Found'

Few years back when we were trying for school admissions for our daughter, we did what we usually do when we move to a new city.

Identify the top 3 schools in the city as per our requirements & then pursue them through calls, visits & Emails. And when I say emails, I am guilty of the fact that I bombard them with follow up emails - so much so that I'm also a wee bit embarrassed in hindsight. -#perseverance

So, yes after a lot of follow ups & effort, we got through 2 schools from the list & chose the 1 that we felt right. I did pursue the 3rd school for a while even after that but then eventually gave up as there was no response to some of the emails that I had sent to them lately! Every time I saw their school bus, I wondered why they hadn't responded. - #wonder

Cut to: last week, when I was clearing my inbox of unwanted mails to make some space. An UNREAD email dated Feb' 2020 from ' 'that' particular school sitting pretty in my inbox. It read : Entrance test for std. 3 and the other details followed in the mail. I don't know HOW I missed it I'm still wondering!!!

I felt soooo many emotions at that moment- joy, regret, irresponsibility, anger, fate etc etc

But the one thing that the mail brought me was - CLOSURE.

CLOSURE. It's such an important aspect of our lives in whatever we do. It's not just limited to banks doing it every March or a sunset every evening :)

We all need #closure. When you flip a #coin and wait for it to land, head or tails?? A chat with the customer service mgr. which asks us to 'end chat' to mk sure that our issue is resolved. Or when you're reading a book & you can't wait to get to the end? A movie or a series which has a sequel or movies with abrupt endings! Don't they leave us wondering? Trust me, the " To be continued....." isn't exciting AT ALL. Don't we all wait till the end in a movie hall till the credits show up..we don't even wanna miss the behind the scenes. - Conclusions

And it doesn't just end there.

Even in #relationships and #friendships, we all need #closure.

Who knows it better than a lover who just went down on his knees & proposed to the person they love!! Haan ki Haan? ;) (love that song)

Many times we drift apart in friendships & we wonder why! And we keep thinking if it was the distance, the lack of communication, a new place or just nothing at all. Nothing happened.. nothing said. That's because there wasn't a #closure.

Break ups happen -sometimes cos ppl. fall out of #love, move on, find somebody else etc. Again, no #closure. What wasn't enough, what went so wrong & the whys aren't always discussed. I've come across so many unhealed people who feel that a closure would've been better.

Probably we are conditioned that way. We need a conclusion. We've been taught to conclude a letter, an essay, an answer, a theorem, a sum with a concluding remark, paragraph, hence proved. The ' the end' & the curtains finally fall is what we wait for!!

What we need to remind ourselves & accept is that closure doesn't always come in the way we expect it to be!

It can also be :

Feedback

The distance

The lack of effort

Silence

To be continued..
Until next time.......

.....
OR, on the flip side
An UNREAD #email.
It's like a love letter lost in the mail and finally delivered to your mailbox on a Friday afternoon when you're not even thinking about it.
And You cry a little, take a deep breath & smile at the same time! :) Finally!!

23

The Pride, The Passion, The Game!

Yesterday was a rollercoaster of emotions that seemed to ripple across the entire nation. The day kicked off with an infectious buzz—a palpable excitement that hung in the air like the aroma of a freshly brewed morning coffee. Enthusiasm was rampant; prayers whispered into the winds, plans meticulously coordinated, and stocks replenished, not just of essentials, but of something equally vital for the occasion—booze! There was a certain charm in the preparations: faces adorned with vibrant paints, flags waving proudly, and the shared anticipation of what lay ahead.

Social media became a bustling hub, narrating every minuscule detail. From the glamorous arrivals and departures of celebrities at airports & 'airport looks' to condominiums & houses decking up for extravagant screenings, it felt as though the entire country was a part of this collective experience. India proudly showcased its prowess—Surya Kirans dancing across the sky, embellished with laser lights, marking a celebration that echoed unity and hope.

The day wasn't immune to setbacks, and while it's easy to delve into the intricacies of what went wrong and how it could have been different, I found myself drawn to something profound amidst the swirl of emotions.

Cricket, undeniably a religion in India, had once again played with our feelings. As a viewer, my emotions took me on a journey—I felt excitement at the beginning, sadness, a deep sense of disappointment, and even anger at times.

Yet, amidst this emotional whirlwind, one sentiment stood tall, distinct, and unwavering—PRIDE. It was as though, in the midst of the chaos and the rollercoaster of feelings, there remained this steadfast beacon of pride in being a part of something larger than ourselves.

There's a unique camaraderie that sports, particularly cricket in India fosters among us. It's not just about the game; it's about the emotions it stirs, the unity it fosters, and the pride it instills in millions.

Yesterday wasn't just about what unfolded on the field; it was a reminder of how intertwined our identities are with the spirit of the game.

As I reflect on yesterday's emotional turmoil, I realize that in this mosaic of feelings, PRIDE shone the brightest. It was a reminder that regardless of the outcome, our unity, our hope, and our shared experiences bind us together as a nation, unyielding and resolute.

Mood: zindagi ki yahi reet hai....

24

God Believing: A New Vocabulary for Faith

God fearing' - A word which has been a part of our vocabulary and a term used for/by people who are religiously/spiritually inclined.

Dictionary meaning: 'earnestly religious'

I, myself have been using it for the longest time that I can remember but recently, I had an Edison moment & I thought to myself: Why was a word like God fearing coined in the 1st place? I get the point about the ancient times - fearing forces of nature etc etc. But that was then!

What's the point of being scared of something/someone and following them out of fear? Isn't it dictatorship? I'm sure God isn't fascist! Something as positive & pious as God cannot be associated with a not so *positive word such as fear! It reminds me of those Whatsapp forwards where you're asked to send to atleast 10 people else this n that!*

That's being unfair to God himself. I'm sure this is not the way he wants us to meet him.

How about 'God believing' instead?

Doesn't that make it sound more convincing, full of faith and reassuring?

Addressing someone's religious/spiritual inclination and dedication as God fearing isn't the right way to project/say it.

Not sure if Oxford dictionary would really change it anytime soon :) but how about changing it to 'God believing ' from now atleast in our everyday vocabulary.

Constant reinforcement in our daily lives would mean clouds of faith, showers of beliefs and fragrance of devotion and piousness all around!

So, next time you see a person who is spiritually inclined - let's use 'God believing'.

If at all we need to fear something, let it be our actions & words. :)

Mood: Emotional.

#justsaying #randommusings

25

Of Tea, Paranthas, and the Resolution to Pause

The final countdown to another year! It's that season when we juggle reflections on the year gone by with the enthusiastic planning of the year about to unfold. – Resolutions!

If I could put the past year in a nutshell then – it was surely a whirlwind of learning curves, moments of introspection and running to follow and stick to 'schedule.' - Commitments!

Between job commitments, household chores (that seem to multiply like rabbits), being a chauffeur to hobby classes (seriously, I could give competition to an Uber driver!), projects, exams, and the extra-curricular activities that take on a life of their own. Amidst all this, my humble cup of tea transformed from piping hot to lukewarm and breakfast resembled an arctic expedition's remnants. - Realizations!

And when I look back, I realise that amidst all these scheduled marvels, there's a missing link called 'ME-time'. You know where self-grooming isn't a pending task and where I drink my tea while it's actually steaming with enthusiasm just like a 2-year-old's excitement on seeing bubbles being blown in the air! - Expectations!

So, here I am, trying to do the year-end ritual - making a resolution. No, not the clichéd 'hit the gym every day' kind (although kudos to those who conquer that mountain!).

Mine is the "I will rescue my tea from the fate of going lukewarm, eat my paranthas while the butter melts on them, and finally prioritize self-care"! Yes, that also includes applying the 'very expensive' night cream before going to bed instead of letting it sit pretty on my dressing table!

Because it's high time I hit the pause button. It's about turning the 'warm' moments into 'hot' ones and bidding farewell to procrastination.

So, for all those of you out there who like to sip your Tea hot:

Here's to 2024 filled with piping hot tea/coffee, breakfasts eaten at a leisurely pace, and self-care routines that make us feel like royalty amidst the madness.

May the only thing that's warm in 2024 be: WARM hugs and the WARMTH of relationships!

Current mood: Ek garam chai ki pyaali ho……. Koi usko 'Peene' wali ho!

26

From Bow and Arrows to TV Shows

In the mosaic of our childhood recollections, one memory that is common among us all, especially the 80's children is the golden era of #Doordarshan- wrapped in nostalgia!

For many of us, #Doordarshan wasn't just a channel; it was our ONLY portal to the enchanting world of cinema. And amidst the handful of programs that graced our #television sets, there were a few that are etched in our hearts till today - still comes up many a times as fond memories with our family & friends and sometimes as a reference in our lecture about the 'problem of plenty' with our children.

#Television back then was meant for "Family viewing" and literally so! There was no content which needed parenteral controls, pins etc.

Take, for example, #Chitrahaar- a kaleidoscope of movie melodies where romantic songs had 2 flowers coming together. A neat and clean, melodious window of 15-30 minutes. Period. - REGULATION.

Then there were the solemn echoes of the news bulletin. Those newsreaders and anchors from yesteryears held a certain mystique, captivating our young minds and igniting aspirations within us. The news readers and anchors back then inspired many of us to become news readers when we grew up! INSPIRATION.

I recall my sister inspired by newsreaders, one with a crisp sari and a rose near her ear! She would drape herself in mom's dupatta, sit upright with a newspaper in hand, and mimic the poised delivery of the newsreaders on screen.

And finally, there was Ramanand Sagar's #Ramayana, a timeless epic for which we would wait all week!

In those simpler times, Sunday mornings held a special charm. The streets lay deserted, and anticipation filled the air. Neighbours would gather in each other's houses. Just like telephones, not every household had a television set. So, mostly padosi ka TV was as good as your TV.

And then as the clock struck 9 AM, "Mangal bhavan amangal haari" filled our homes. It was an experience that was more than just entertainment.

Looking back, I realize how fortunate we were to have learned the story of Ramayana through the lens of Ramanand Sagar's vision on TV. Unlike children today, who are confined to the pages of textbooks, we had the privilege of witnessing the epic unfold before our very eyes. And it didn't end there.

The magic of #Ramayana followed us in our aangans & our pretend plays! With bow and arrows made of Jhaadu ka seek (yes, there were no hard plastic brooms back then) So, with that jhaadu ka teela bent carefully and a thin thread joining 2 ends, the other Teela for arrows and a newspaper rolled to make an arrow holder - punched in and joined with threads. And we were all Lord Ram and Lakshman.

Not sure if anyone ever wanted to be Raavanaa but SIta maiya was in great demand. Whether they wanted to be the rani version with all maalas and dupattas from our mom's wardrobe or the exile version in a humble orange sari /dupatta, depended on the mood, I think :)- IMAGINATION.

Those were the days when we weren't really spoilt for choice in any way!

Cut to today: where even though the channels may have multiplied, and the choices expanded, there will always be a corner of our hearts reserved for those cherished moments spent in the warm embrace of #Doordarshan, where innocence thrived, and nostalgia STILL reigns supreme.

Mood: Yaadon ki baaraat...

27

From "Hamri Atariya pe aaja re" to swipe right!

————♡————

I asked Alexa - to play music I like. By now, I think Alexa knows me a bit more than I would like her to (eye roll), but in any case, Alexa started playing songs from the romance genre. The genre was right, but the choice of songs that came next compelled me to ponder, and here I am, putting it on pen and paper. (More like screen and keyboard)

The definition of love and romance (which has inspired many poets, artists, and dreamers for centuries) has transformed over time. The dynamics...or if I can use the word the ways of expressing love and attraction have evolved from the subtle exchanges of glances to the passionate embraces depicted in modern songs. For Good or bad? Let's keep that debate/discussion for another time. :)

I may sound like I belong to the era that I am speaking about - that's not true. But yes, the songs, the movies and many stories about 'hamare zamaane mein" I have heard from friends n family have made me believe that the dynamics of love and attraction have changed.

In the stories from the "Hamare zamaane mein" era, love was often communicated through shy glances and unspoken gestures - something to the effect of "Aankhon hee Aankhon mein ishara ho gaya" or Begum Akhtar's soulful rendition of "Hamri Atariya pe aaja re sawariya , dekha dekhi tanik hoyi jaaye". It beautifully encapsulates the essence of quiet yearning and unexpressed desires. Even in the movies, Love was a delicate dance, where every glance held a world of meaning, and every interaction was steeped in anticipation. In those days, love blossomed in the flutter of eyelashes and the brush of fingertips, and a mere wave could send hearts aflutter!

Cut to today's day and age. Where love and attraction are often depicted with boldness and sensuality in movies, songs and even social media! Which then is obviously replicated in real life. What has happened in the process is that the charm of the anticipation of a phone call is replaced by the instant gratification of blue ticks, right swipes, video calls and true caller IDs of today's age! But still, the wait for the phone to ring, or the thrill of receiving a handwritten letter, or gradually knowing a person 'in person' (unlike thru social media) is unmatched! I have quite a few friends on my friend list from 'that era', and I am sure that they can surely confirm this.

It is something like comparing a slow-cooked meal on a traditional chulha in earthen pots to a quick one in the microwave or a gas stove! Sure, the latter is more convenient, but the flavour, nourishment and aroma are unmatched by the former! There's a certain depth, a richness to the old ways that seem to elude our fast-paced lives.

Well, obviously, love is love, and it definitely remains a personal and subjective experience. But as I ponder over the 'then and now', let us cherish the memories of yesteryears and never forget the magic of "Aankhon hee Aankhon mein ishara ho gaya" and the timeless allure of "Hamri Atariya" by Begum Akhtar while embracing the complexities of modern romance. :)

On Loop : Yeh shaam mastani...

28

Living in a Sitcom: Who Are You in Everyone's Story?

Watching so many series on Netflix, it got me thinking that we are all living in a sitcom where everyone has their own version of us! Sometimes I wonder about the different roles I play in everyone's story. It's like being the star of a show you didn't even audition for!

In some people's tales, I'm the villain: courtesy, my evil laugh and dramatic thunderclap. Or maybe something else?

In others, I'm practically an angel: halo and all, sprinkling kindness like it's confetti.

But here's the good news: while you know what really defines you, all of these roles have more to do with them than it is to do with you. The thing is, everyone's perception of you is like their own personal Instagram *filter—totally based on their upbringing, beliefs, and experiences.*

Your infectious energy? Some find it charming; others find it as welcome as a Monday morning alarm! Aargh. Yes- that's the reaction.

Your emotional side? Some see it as vulnerability; others see it as an open invitation to be themselves & connect with you.

Your assertiveness? Some think you're rude, others applaud your self-respect.

Your frank nature? Maybe perceived as blunt/ overconfident but maybe an inspiration for those that see you as calling a spade, a spade.

To cut the long story short, It's all about their perspective, not your reality!

Trying to control how others see you is like trying to control the weather (specially Bangalore weather)—pointless and frustrating.

The only thing that really counts when the day ends and the credits roll is how you see yourself! :)

So, embrace your role, whether you're the hero, the villain, or the comedic sidekick, and keep doing you. After all, you're the one living your story.

Quoting a phrase from Ramcharit manas:

जाकी रही भावना जैसी, प्रभु मूरत देखी तनि तैसी.

Mood: hum hain rahi pyaar ke....

29
The swing

───────❦───────

A poem I learned in Class 6 has left an indelible mark on my memory. Ever since, whenever I see a swing, I can't help but recite those timeless lines by Robert Louis Stevenson: "How do you like to go up in a swing, up in the air so high?" I remember also reciting this poem for my entrance interview at a school. (Yes, I did get through :)

But this swing I'm talking about now sings a different tune.

This swing (my favorite place in my house) has been my confidant, my retreat, and my sanctuary. It has heard secrets, soaked up many laughs, and been there through countless heart-to-heart conversations with family and friends. It has been the launch pad for my mornings and the perfect place to unwind in the evenings. We've shared many cups of tea and witnessed some truly wild parties together. It has seen joy, laughter, madness, happy and 'high' moments, and everything in between.

More than just a swing, it has been my companion through the highs and lows. It has weathered my mood 'swings' with grace even when my mood would swing in the wrong direction ;). Just sitting here, perched on it, I've had moments of deep reflection, daydreams, and pure contentment. It has soaked it all up from sunrise sips to late-night parties, the rain drops, the breeze, the poetry, Google meetings, the music: this swing has seen it all.

Today, as I reflect back on the times spent, I hold on to the memories, the clarity, and the joy it has gifted me and I am again reminded of Stevenson's words. This time, they resonate with a deeper meaning: "Up in the air and over the wall, till I can see so wide, rivers and trees and cattle and all, over the countryside."

This swing has given me a view not just of my surroundings but of my inner landscape.

Here's to the swing that held more than just my weight—it held my dreams, my thoughts, and a piece of my heart.

Mood: Girls like to swing ;)

30
Love at first Insight!

I am currently reading a book which talks about love in the context of spiritual and transformative love rather than just initial attraction. And it got me to write this piece!

I think love at first sight is overrated.

I'm not trying to steal the thunder from those who swear by it. I'm sure Cupid has his moments of precision. But ...ummmm... love at First Sight is hyped up primarily because of Hollywood, Bollywood & romance novels. Probably more than the current craze for avocado, chia seeds & vegan food! They've pumped this whole concept like what protein shakes would do to a gym enthusiast or maybe the new age lipsticks that make your lips pout! Really?? *eyeroll*

This made me think of scenarios of love at first manys (if that's a word at all!)

How about Love at First Argument! There's something magical about that first heated debate where sparks fly, voices raise, and suddenly, you discover that pineapple on pizza is actually not a bad combination (I know many ppl like it but I don't like it and because I'm the author of this article, I will give this example. Period - Stubborn me!)

This kind of love also reminds me of group discussion during our MBA interviews & GD rounds & I know of someone who share this - Love at first GD. ;)

How about Love at First Inside Joke? That moment when two people laugh at something that would make absolutely no sense to anyone else, and suddenly, you're in a secret club of two. The kind of love that starts with a shared giggle or an eye signal and snowballs into a lifetime of private punchlines!

How about Love at First Un-Awkward Silence? It's that comfortable pause in conversation where neither of you feels the need to fill the space with meaningless chatter. You both just exist together, content and connected. This is the silence where you realize that maybe you've found your person—the one who doesn't make you feel the need to babble about the weather or make forceful conversations.

And then, there's Love at First Support Through Hardships. It's easy to be smitten when things are all rainbows and unicorns but it's the person who stands by you handing you tissues. Sob!

Love at First Shared Passion. Discovering someone who shares your enthusiasm for a particular hobby, interest, and feeling an immediate bond over your mutual dedication.

And I am sure there are many more love at firsts.....

But whatever your first may be, here's a funny thing I read somewhere and agreed to. 'If you really want to test your relationship's durability, hand your partner a phone with slow internet or argue about the perfect air conditioning temperature. If they can survive those ordeals without turning into a rage monster, you've got yourself a keeper!' LOL.

So here's to celebrating all the "firsts" that truly matter—the glance, the hobbies & interests, the ones that deepen with time, laughter, and the shared endurance of life's little challenges.

Because in the end, it's not about how love begins, but how beautifully it EVOLVES.

Mood: Love Me For a Reason

91

31

Zindagi ka Ganit

Our latest movement made me realize how important it is to declutter. Our homes, our lives and most importantly our minds!

As kids when we start learning #Math , what comes right after counting 1-10 is addition followed by subtraction. While addition is all simple, the less popular cousin of addition - Subtraction isn't really fun! 2 apples plus 2 more apples equals a happy snack time. But when it comes to subtraction, 2 apples minus 1 apple—suddenly snack time feels less exciting. Who wants to part with an apple, right? Okay let's make that a chocolate muffin! I can understand that apple doesn't sound that tempting! Now read that again with a muffin!

Anyways, subtraction isn't just about math problems! It's a secret superpower that we can wield to add more joy, peace, and sanity to our chaotic/busy lives. Recent realization for me!

Our lives nowadays are a crash course in addition—adding bills, responsibilities, classes, meetings, EMIs and I'm not even getting to the grey hair & the dark circles! Argh.

The point is : How about adding a bit of subtraction to our lives? (+) (-) = minus

Remember that committee or a whatsapp group you joined because you felt obliged to? Subtract it. Free up your schedule/phone memory and reclaim your time. Less time in meetings, group discussions, whatsapp messages- more time for Netflix or maybe to exercise! (Achha chalo, atleast pretending to!)

I often make a to-do list and wonder who is really going 'TO-DO' all of this?! So, I then sit and cross off the non-priority. Do I really need to label my spice rack today?? No, I do not. Subtract. Feels lighter!

My laptop desktop is full of icons. Each time I switch it on, i feel I must organize and clean but then work takes over! Also my inbox, I need to unsubscribe to the list of unwanted mailers! So, I took a day and sat to clear the clutter. It was both literal and metaphorical.

Less chaos, more zen. Icing on the cake was a mail I found that made me smile :) the same feeling when u find money in ur jeans pockets! ;)

Subtracting caffeine sounds directly proportional to productivity, but sometimes less tea/coffee equals more sleep which equals a happier you. Or, on the flip side, adding just the right amount of caffeine can prevent you from turning into a zombie before 10 AM. Balance, people, Balance.

So, let's subtract the chaos and add more peace & laughter to our daily calculations. Like #Friendships, #hobbies, #vacations, #fitnessregimes...

May our lives be simpler like 1 to 10 and our tea cups just the right size!

And remember, don't let the coffee/tea get cold. :)

MOOD: zindagi ek safar hai suhaana....

32

Tick mark

The other day when I was correcting my daughter's work, I went through what she had done and told her that she's done a good job. Pat came the reply - but you've not corrected it! I said, I've gone through & it seems fine. But Where's the tick mark? Hmmmm....

The tick mark has been with us since our childhood.

Only the colors have changed over the years. From pencil grey to red to blue!!

As kids when our books would be corrected, the red tick marks meant correct answers. A star obviously was the icing on the cake but the tick mark was the confirmation to things done right!

What often proceeded the red tick mark was self correction done in pencil, only to be confirmed/

95

validated later by the teacher.

Little did we know as children that the same tick mark would become an essential part of our lives, Only in another color -Blue & another medium- digital.

When I came to know about a brand called Nike, I made a mental note of the logo - the one with a tick. Much later, I think during my graduation in one of the Philip kotler books, I learned the term is actually 'swoosh!' I'm sure a big brand like Nike also has insecurities from this recent tick mark which has taken the world by storm. And as if that was not enough, the blue color has made it even more complicated.

It's taken away the art of patience from us! The word 'thehraav' which is already lacking in our lives given the pace of today's world - the tick mark has robbed us totally of it.

The core of all this is obviously 'expectations' - but let's keep this one for a separate blog some othe time!

So there are levels to it.

1 tick - omg! Not delivered??? Why?? Why? Wifi check. Data check.

2 ticks- aah! Finally delivered. Let's wait for the reply. Tick tick tick tock.....

Blue tick- what?? Read and not replied? Something wrong? Forgetting me? Me not important? All ok, I hope? Waiting..... waiting.... waiting...... & drafting a stinker already, breakup text ready to send.... blah blah.

Note to self for all the above scenarios: Take a deep breath. RELAX.

I am not even getting to the setting where ppl keep read receipts off! I read somewhere which said ' never trust ppl who keep the blue tick option off'- m.not in the mood to debate that rt now. So chuck!

So, yeah the tick mark which signifies things done right is, in my opinion responsible for so many wrongs that it has brought to our lives - anxiety, unrest, doubt, fear, bitterness, unnecessary assumptions blah blah blah. And I take the liberty to speak on behalf of most of us, atleast our generation!

Wondering about the day when a normal greeting which has seen many transitions from :

How are you?

What's new?

How you doing?

WhatsUp?

becomes

WhatsApp??

Mood: not in the mood for music today! ;)

33

Push or Pull

So it was my first class at Aqua Zumba!

Most of the exercises were with the noodle—those long cylindrical foam rods! It was either #PUSH or #PULL, both of which require a great deal of effort underwater!

Each time I stopped in between, our instructor would say, "Don't quit, but don't hurt yourself!"

Come to think of it, that's what it is about: #Push and #Pull - the way we live our lives and the things we do!

NO. I AM NOT TALKING ABOUT THE PUSH AND PULL NOTIFICATIONS ON OUR #SMARTPHONES! That's a trap (confessions of a shopaholic)

The #Push is basically "Don't quit" #pull is "Don't get hurt"

Can almost visualise tug of war no?!

In life, we all need to push ourselves most of the time. Whether it is :

pushing ourselves out of bed on a Monday morning..Yawwwwn

pushing our lil ones literally out of the door to catch the school bus!

cheering for them to push just a little more cos they're a few steps away from the finish line.

pushing yourself to the gym....more like dragging!

pushing a work deadline to the next day ;) procrastination is real!

OR

pushing a baby out....! well..... much like coconut out of nostrils!

Some people be like: "too posh to push!"

And then the #Pull.

Pulling ourselves back to save us from the hurt, both physically and #emotionally' - the keyword here is the latter!

Pull back your emotions to stay detached/for sanity's sake.

Pull back the urge to type that looooong message and just reply with an #OK

Pulling back words to avoid a conflict

pulling your sibling's hair in the middle of the fight (growing up tales!)

OR

Pulling back your hair into a bun before the big cleaning day at home - yeah, that's me today! ;)

It is all about the balance - it's tricky and delicate.

In most situations, I don't even know whether to push or pull. Sometimes, I choose the wrong one, only to learn later—much like those signs on the door that say pull on one side and push on the other—I always get it wrong the first time. ALWAYS.

But with so many movements to different cities, I think I am now getting a hang of the push-pull.

I am learning to remove all the things and emotions that #pull me back—memories, nostalgia, weather, routine, house etc. This obviously doesn't mean you forget the friends you made & the good times you've had—YOU DoN't . But then, don't let those #memories pull you back from making new connections & moving on.

The #Push... well... pushing myself to embrace a new routine, humid weather (haha), new friends, and new energy

In the process, you sweat it out a little (quite literally), but then that's what we call - keep moving forward :)

So, the next time you see the #pull and #push sign on those doors - remember me :)

Mood : yunhi chala chal raahi ..yunhi chala chal. kitni haseen hai yeh dunia.

34

Every #Pillow Has a Story!

As I lay my head down each night, a thousand thoughts run through my mind - from the mundane to the profound. And amidst all this, one constant companion is my humble #pillow

It's not just fluff, fabric and feathers! For most of us, our #pillow has seen it all – the midnight musings, the epiphanies, the heartfelt sobs, and the joyous giggles!

Well, obviously a #pillow is known for providing physical comfort & support (we'll talk about special pillows for spondylitis sufferers later, btw, there are special ones for that too). But have we ever thought about the mental comfort & support that it provides?

It's like a therapist who never judges and always listens! Our pillows have seen it all - Soaking up tears during heartbreaks, loss or simply venting out pent-up emotions. So many love letters must've been penned *lying on pillows. Muffling screams of frustration, and cushioning our heads through countless sleepless nights, our late-night confessions, our secrets, exam revisions, our dreams, our most intimate thoughts! And not to forget the growing up years where it has been both, a weapon & shield during our #PILLOW FIGHTS - playing both offense and defense & leaving us with laughter, the giggles & the soft thud!*

It's the Watson to our Sherlock, the Robin to our Batman, the Pooh to the Piglet. It's seen us through moments of brilliance, realisation and confessions!

Every #pillow has a story - of comfort, companionship, and countless dreams.

So, the next time you rest your head, try and listen closely, you might just hear it whispering back, "Goodnight, sleep tight, I've got your back (quite literally) ." :) Just like a good friend !

Happy friendships Day!

Mood: Jab koi baat bigad jaaye, Jab koi mushkil padd jaaye tum dena saath Mera.....

35

Scribbles, Tweets, and Heartbeats: The Journey of #Words

"You have a way with #words" "shabdon ki dhani"- something I hear very often & it feels good. Maybe it's true! But come to think of it, aren't we all made up of #words?

Just like they say, everything 'around' us is science- everything 'about' us is #Words!!

Whether it's a prayer we say, an introduction, an explanation, a confession, a proposal, a resume, a matrimonial, an invite, the mantras we chant, a simple wish, movie dialogue, raising a toast, or just thinking......... all defined by alphabets sewn together into #words! Words have an uncanny ability to connect us. They bridge the gaps between us or maybe *create :-O*

#Words are like the Swiss Army knives of our lives. They can start revolutions and mend broken relationships. We use them to express, impress, motivate........... Words can indeed create an uproar. The famous idiom " Look before you leap, think before you speak" - so true!

But in the age of social media, the adage "Think before you speak" has evolved into "Think before you post." A hasty tweet can immortalize your missteps, turning you into an internet sensation for all the wrong reasons—"gone viral", as they call it. This could turn out more draining and damaging than an actual viral ! Future generations might study your blunder like a modern-day Shakespearean tragedy or a case study in marketing books—who knows! ;)

*With texting/Whatsapp becoming the prime mode of exchange and nowadays being preferred over a phone call, it's become all the more important for us to understand that #words carry weight, echoing in the hearts of those who read them - sometimes for a lifetime. The age-old saying that words, once spoken, cannot be taken back is only partially true nowadays with the "Delete for everyone" option on WhatsApp - both good & bad but either ways, the intent shows! *eyeroll**

So, the next time you're about to unleash your verbal arsenal, take a moment to pause. Think about the weight your #words carry. Choose them wisely and give them life with an intention whose future isn't " "Delete for everyone"

Because #words have the power to uplift, connect, heal, and, yes, take someone's breath away—or their heart. (Ronan Keating style ;) For words, once spoken, live on forever—etched in print, engraved in memories (now also, phone memory), and carried in hearts.

Mood: It's only #words, and #words are all I have to take your heart away......

And as I finish writing this, I'm reminded of the movie 'Music and Lyrics', in which Hugh Grant and Drew Barrymore find themselves in a creative whirlwind, trying to craft the perfect song. In their journey, we see the power of #words unfold. Alex's music might catch your ear first, but it's Sophie's lyrics that give the song its heart and soul. :) #justsaying

36

Weather or Whether......

The last two months here in Mumbai have been all about grey skies and pitter patters! No sunshine days! Am I cribbing? Ahem.... ! maybe.

Now, as Mumbai almost wraps up the monsoon in another month and gears up to give us ABIGSTICKYHUG (sorry for that—letters tend to stick together because of the humidity; it's a Mumbai thing! ;), it got me thinking about something deeper—just like different places have their unique weather, we too have ours—those that mirror our emotions and moods!

Imagine this: there's a little meteorologist constantly forecasting our inner weather. Sometimes, it's bright and sunny, with joy and happiness overflowing like a perfectly brewed cup of tea on a Sunday morning. Those are the days when everything seems right, and you do everything with a smile—even if that means doing truckloads of laundry! Aargh.

And then there is the thunder and lightning. Ah, those electrifying moments of anger and irritation. Every little thing sets you off like a firecracker. Your patience wears thin, and you find yourself snapping at everything and everyone. While the housemates are waiting for the storm to pass.

Then there are the rainy days. No, I don't mean the gentle, romantic rain that makes you want to cosy up with a book! I am talking about the torrential downpour of pent-up emotions - ready to burst into tears at the slightest provocation. You try to keep it together, but the dam breaks and the flood of emotions is unstoppable. PMS-ing, in our case! hmph.

But guess what? Without the rain, there would be no RAINBOWS! :-) Ah, the glorious rainbows of hope and smiles that appear after the storm. These days are when everything feels possible, and you're filled with optimism and positivity. Hit the gym, I say!!

On some days, the cold creeps in—not the nip in the air of a winter morning, but the bone-freezing numbness of indifference. It's the kind of cold that makes you go through days without really feeling anything. Maybe a human popsicle ;)

Then there are the days of drought. These are the boring days when everything feels dry and lifeless. Your patience, energy, and enthusiasm are all but depleted, and you wander through your daily routine disinterested. Zombie.

Basically, our internal weather shifts based on our situations, surroundings, circumstances & affects everything about & around us.

So, the next time the weather inside you changes, don't shy away from it. It's high time we learn to embrace the sunshine, dance in the rain, weather the storms and look for the rainbows.

Let's begin with 'Being True' to our innerselves kyunki 'beimaan toh sirf mausam Hota hai' ;)

Mood: aaj mausam bada... beimaan hai bada....

37

50 Shades Of Grey !

Ha! The title got you. Didn't it ? ;)

'Hook' as we call it in the mktg lingo.

Now read!!

For the longest time I have been a believer, a preacher and a practitioner of "Either Or" , "This or That" " Black or white" and nothing in between! But then there is a space between the black n white & thats what is the Grey area!

For me, it always had to be either right OR wrong, like something OR detest, want it OR not, say it as is #nofilter OR keep it all within etc etc. - No grey areas!

But then I realised that it doesnt work like that. For eg. my choice of coffee needn't always be Black OR milky white, neither cold nor piping hot! What if I'd Like it to be luke warm with a hint of foam on top and a bit of chocolate too??

Basically, the more I think about it, life obviously isn't always lived and experienced in absolutes! Most of our lives happen in the Grey areas - surrounded by "what ifs" "maybes" "lemme think about it" etc

Decisions dont always have to be as crisp as a fresh stack of JK COPIER Printer paper. Situations like, Want to move to a new city? Yes or no. A new job offer? Take it or leave it. Most of these answers and decisions aren't served on a right or wrong platter. It's in a.perpetual shade of grey leaving us to figure it out by weighing the pros and cons & prioritizing, deciding what's best for us! The inner voice will always be 'I hope I'm making the right decison' - only to unfold as time goes by!

We maybe tested, refined, and sometimes... left confused. These in betweens is where we grow!

Sure it's frustrating at times. Maybe also makes us anxious and restless! But unknowingly teaches us patience & we learn to embrace , accept and just be!

But you know what??

As much as we all love Clarity, what I've come to realise is that there is a lot that happens in the "in betweens" - The grey area as we call it!

It's where you'll find the best stories, the"remember-when-I-was-indecisive" tales that will keep your friends entertained for hours & you will be narrating the same to your children & your grandchildren sitting on an easy chair, sipping your neither Black nor milky coffee, with a dash of foam and chocolate- served Luke warm, just the way you like it :)

38

Mice. Mountains. Mindset.

I am not a TV buff, but when I do, I love watching Tom & Jerry. It leaves me guffawing! You know the drill - Tom will chase Jerry! Basically, Tom is 'conditioned' to chase Jerry. But Jerry flips the script. He doesn't run in fear like he's 'supposed' to—he fights back with frying pans and mousetraps and sometimes even a piano. Ouch!

Since childhood we're conditioned to pursue things, relationships, emotions, behaviour in a certain set way! Remember the scenery we all drew as children? The mountain range whichh was always brown with the sun peeking shyly from behind. A river snaked through the peaks, a lonely hut with a perfectly square window and a broccoli head/coconut tree as if it had signed a lifetime lease on that spot. It didn't matter where we lived or what landscapes we'd actually seen on our travels. This was how we were conditioned to define 'scenery.' It was a template passed down like a sacred handbook!

We grew up with templates. Not just for drawing but for thinking, reacting, and living. A good girl/boy does this, success looks like that, and problems should be solved in this specific way, relationships should be this, emotions should ne expressed a certain way, see people as competitors, someone gets the job we wanted, someone achieves what we haven't. ...etc etc etc

The scenery we drew as kids wasn't wrong. It was just what we knew, were told! We were never taught to redraw, rethink, and redefine. We stuck to that 'ideal' scenery in our heads because it's Familiar. Safe. Predictable.

What if we were asked to draw a new scenery for ourselves? One where success isn't jet-setting across the globe but finding time to stroll barefoot on soft grass. One where relationships don't fit into neat labels but are defined by the books you share and the laughs you exchange with some sarcasm and banter thrownm in. One where the mountains are green & the river bends unpredictably, and the tree? Ummm.... it's not a tree at all...

It's a giant mushroom because.... because. because!!!!

Real life happens outside that template and those templates we were handed are meant to be questioned, pushed and when necessary even wiped out!

So grab that crayon and start drawing your own scenery. Paint the sun wherever you want it & let the trees be swaying and drooping or let it be a sapling! And don't forget to add a mouse wielding a frying pan. After all, we could all use a little Jerry energy in our lives. isn't it? :)

39

The Little Red Man.

I saw this LITTLE RED MAN standing in a corner at the post office. It reminded me of a little boy at a birthday party standing there with an upside-down smiley face :-(because he couldn't gather enough candies when the piñata broke. Feeling left out, holding an empty bag.

'Maybe next time', says the Mumma! Sure, this little boy will grow and by the next birthday party be able to figure his way out and collect more candies! Let's wait for him to turn a year older! :)

The boy will grow 'older' embracing the future, while the RED letterbox grows 'OLDER' slipping further into the past.

But this LITTLE RED MAN..... I don't know if there will be a next time for him.

There was a time when this box wasn't just a box. It was a storyteller....a keeper of secrets.... a vessel of emotions.. with sooooo many stories to tell! He stood proud in almost every corner becoming the silent witness to a world that communicated with ink and paper.

A big-hearted fellow I'm sure or maybe a big belly who held love in carefully folded envelopes, the ink still wet with longing. From announcing births, marriages and sometimes...... ! Carrying the future of so many of us with job applications... college acceptances and money orders. Each time a letter was dropped it was he who gave them wings sending them to places far and wide. -

The dakiya daak wala's facilitator of bakshish!

But then came the Email.

..ahem! His shiny heir. Sleek, fast, efficient (sounds similar to a FEMALE no? ;). The one who is fast, who doesn't misplace or lose a thing, keeps a record of everything etc etc. And so the LITTLE RED MAN was left standing in a forgotten corner gazing longingly at the hustle and bustle he once knew.

But you know what?! Things and memories like these don't fade. They linger quietly, whispering their tales to those who care to listen. The LITTLE RED MAN reminds us of simpler times and of a world where patience was a virtue and the handwritten word was king. When love travelled openly expressed in heartfelt words on postcards and inland letters & we waited with bated breath.

As I paused to click a picture of the letterbox, I couldn't help but wonder whether it envies the email. Or does it simply smile knowing that it lived in a time when love was handwritten, stamped and sealed with a kiss! :)

40

Friday Feels & Table Tales

It was one of those impromptu Fridays when my friends and I decided to finally meet! My friend and I have been friends of 20+ years & yes I like to mention it repeatedly & we wear that number like a badge. Thank you very much! Old friends, old habits... Pun intended there! ;)

While she was coming straight from work, I wrapped up my WFH Friday with the enthusiasm of a child on the last day of exams!

'Some place else ' at BKC- Cute little place with dim lighting, not so loud music, decent food and a list of pretty- looking colorful cocktails! When asked, if we preferred high chairs or the cozy corner, we chose the high chairs. Remember, Standards & Heels- Always high. ;)

Our Conversations revolved around work, kids & the beautiful chaos of Mumbai life (my fav topic currently. Haha) . We didn't even realize when the tables literally turned ;) and the evening unfolded like a mini-series with each table around us playing its own episode.

The table just across us had a group of young office kids who were there for Yay! its finally friday session. How do I know they were working? They came with their laptop bags, formally dressed, some still finishing work- meeting deadlines probably! It looked like their first jobs - looking at the diligence ;) In that group, we could see some love stories simmering , some glances being exchanged and then there was this "tu apna yaar hai" vibe too! It took us straight back to our first jobs, where ambition and awkwardness were the big A!

To our left was a couple who held hands, they giggled, whispered, blushed and occasionally also fed each other. Definitely NOT MARRIED. Lol. It was the perfect 'Pehla nasha, Pehla khumaar" kinda love and we couldn't help but smile and say, Awwww! The young love... unburdened by grocery lists and EMIs. ;) haha..

Then there was this heavily pregnant woman straight out of work with her colleague. Her classily draped sari is what drew our attention. She spoke in an animated way. Her wide-eyed expressions and dramatic hand movements suggested she was discussing workplace politics.... not too sure but if you know, you know! What was admirable about her was her energy! She was undoubtedly a queen juggling two worlds with flair.

Then of course there were walk ins - girl gang like ours, the selfie clicking group, the "here for gossip" girls, old couples accompanied by their children & grand children.

That outing wasn't just a girl's night out. That evening, we time-travelled! Every table around us was a mirror reflecting who we Were, who we Are, and who we might Become.

It was a letter to our younger selves filled with laughter, nostalgia, and the realization that some stories never get old. They just find new tables to roll on. :)

Here's to strictly Girls' therapy outings and the tables that tell tales.

41

Dear December

It's been 2 days since you arrived. They say, "Save the best for last" and Who would know this better than you?!!! So, how does it feel to be the showstopper of the year & the most sought-after month? Is the pressure of expectations real? I mean...... the countdowns, the reflecting on the year gone by....the planning for the next year...i'm sure it all feels overwhelming no?! Or do you just sit back smiling and sip your hot cocoa surrounded by gingerbread men, candy canes, cookies, and snowflakes? haha... like the head honcho!

As they say, with great power comes great responsibility. ;) You're like the BIG Boardroom where the biggest decisions are made (Read: New Year resolutions), travel itineraries for the next year, Gym regimes etc. The quiet moments when people reflect on the year gone by.....what they gained, what they lost and what they hope to carry into the next year. You own it all with grace!

I really admire you for keeping up with so much with a smile! I get bogged down with 20 unread emails and a to-do list staring at me on a Monday morning! *EYE ROLL*

You truly shine as a host too, with a big belly...errrr... heart! Hosting a month-long party and making room for EVERYONE..... Welcoming Santa and his entourage, the towering Christmas trees, the gingerbread man, the snowflakes, glitters, twinkling lights..... a playlist that has everything from carols to party songs. And how can I forget the secret santas & the letters to Santa - every child's favourite. You turn every moment into a memory. I mean who would even think of making a chimney.... yes, A CHIMNEY a VIP entrance!! You own the number '31' like a star... the one who has redefined the colours Red and white not just as hues but as a mood of joy and celebration.

You truly ARE the GRAND' Finale.... the perfect blend of a graceful Farewell and a Hopeful Hello. :)

So here's to Diva December.....

The Overachiever

The Memory-maker

The Keeper of Promises

The Storyteller

&

The final countdown

P.S. pssst... do you by any chance know whether I'm on the naughty or nice list?

With love,

Me

42

Tag vs. Tug!

The other day, a tag on my new top was irritating me, so I cut it off! Good riddance. Only to realise later that I didn't read the wash instructions on it! Wish I had taken a moment to read it and paid more attention to it...because those little details matter for the fabric to last longer and stay in good condition! (Just like ppl)

And that left me wondering what if we humans also came with care instructions like the ones on clothing labels? Would people then know how to treat each other better and accordingly? We would all fit into different categories with our own specific needs and quirks!

Gentle Handwash. Do not wring or twist! These are the kind of people who are gentle by nature and one wrong word might make them shrink into their shell. Handle with care otherwise they might just unravel. Any exposure to the wrong person or situation can lead to an emotional meltdown. A few kind words might be all it takes to put them back together....but they're are fragile, so best to avoid the Machine wash with them... because some of them may look like they're invincible, but their delicate hearts need soothing......not scrubbing and tumbling.

Then there are some who fit into the 'Dry Clean only' bracket. Just like our fancy party wear. They cant just adjust in any and every social circle. They need safe, trusted spaces..... environments that allow them to feel seen and heard. They're are choosy that way!!

Let's just say they freelance their chattiness and social personality! ;) No shallow talks. Only deep heartfelt conversations with their people. I think that's me!! :)

I think the 'Do not bleach' and 'Avoid direct sunlight' will probably fall into the same category. Any kind of harsh words and statements can leave permanent stains on their souls. These are the overthinkers and overanalysts. They can't handle extreme temperatures (read behaviour) . Too much love & attention can make them get over-involved, and cold behaviour can totally make them distant! Is that also me??? *confused*

Well.... I agree that these tags can sometimes feel irritating and get too much to handle. But instead of cutting them off without a second thought, maybe we can pause for a moment and reflect. After all, we're not just made of cotton or polyester but of emotions and feelings. A.N.D. We all are complex in some way or the other! *Truth*

So, the next time we interact with someone.......even though the tag isn't visible, let's be mindful to treat them with a bit more softness, tenderness, and care.

Because at the end of the day, we're ALL just trying to keep it together.

One gentle wash at a time! :)

43

Chhook-Chook Gaadi

The place where we live in Bangalore has a train track nearby somewhere.

So, the sound of the train, the whistle of the engine is a part of the many other sounds that we hear.

During the day, it gets mixed up with the chirping of the birds, the honking, the engine starting, the dog barking, the chatter of the children in the park, the cooker whistle in the house et all

It's at night that one tends to pay attention to because of the quiet.

Last night, as I lay awake in bed pretty late cos I wasn't getting sleep for some reason. The daily whistle of some late night train brought back many childhood memories. Fond memories... and I wrote this article in my mind last night...and here I am putting it on paper (actually screen) right now.

It took me back to our Summer vacations.

Summer Vacations meant packing hard top bulky suitcases, safar ka khaana, paper soaps, big kool kegs, comics (Walkman came in much later) & the excitement to climb up the steel ladder to get to the top berth.

The highlight of those big bulky suitcases was getting to sit, jump, hop on those suitcases a little harder each time so that mom/dad could close them with the click of those 2 steel panels on both sides.

Journeys meant buying comics & books from the A.H. Wheeler stall at the Railway stations which had all the books and magazines neatly displayed. My sister and I would pick up our favorite Billoo, Pinky, Chacha Choudhary while Mom & Dad would probably pick up a sarita/femina & India today respectively. And oh! Just for recall, Chacha Choudhary is the same guy jiska dimaag computer se bhi tez chalta hai and till a certain age , I used to wonder that volcanoes did erupt cos Sabu ko gussa aata hai!

Safar ka khaana would mostly be parantha, alu bhujia or sometimes karela with achaar. With sheets of newspaper spread on the seat, dinner was laid &

sometimes shared with fellow passengers ?. And most of the times, our co passenger's food looked yummier than ours.

At around 930-10, Khaki colored Duckback pillows would be inflated, we would put our own sheets on the seat. (Sleeping bags came in later when we could travel by A.C.)

The whole compartment's lights were put off with only this faint blue light on & most of the times if the fan would stop working, we would just give it a spin with a pen and there! It worked. Well.... So many would have got their passion to be electrical engineers from this one experience, who knows!?

The windows had 2 shutters – one transparent thick glass for it be put down during rains, storm etc. & the other one was an aluminium shutter with grooves for ventilation, if one didn't want to keep it all open, specially at night to avoid theft.

Kaun sa station hai bhaiya? Train late chal rahi hai kya? Are the 2 statements which helped ppl estimate the time of their arrival at the destination.

The joy of being able to see the other compartments from outside your window, when the train would take a turn or the magic of how the tracks appeared to meet and then separate, is still unmatched. It was nothing less than magic, back then.

All of the above seem to be little things but all of these took me back to the carefree days.

And as I write this, I'm reminded of Robert Brault's famous quote, "Enjoy the little things for one day you may look back and realize they were the big things"

I'm sure that the past year has just made the belief in this quote even stronger for all of us.

And on that note, my heart is longing to sing....

"We're all goin' on a summer holiday
No more workin' for a week or two
Fun and laughter on a summer holiday
No more worries for me or you.................

44
Sunshine shoes!

Recently, my daughter bought a pair of yellow and white checkered shoes with a white sole! They're very cute. We call them sunshine shoes! Let me put a yellow heart emoji for them. . There!!

Given the light color and the love for the new pair, she's over protective...... Constantly bothered about them getting dirty! Walking carefully. Hopping. Jumping to avoid dirt etc etc. Yet, despite her careful choreography, those pristine soles get dirty!! Even though the wet wipes are being used by the dozen, I resist every urge to say "Stop obsessing, it's just dirt! and have decided to keep quiet because giving unsolicited advice is the leading cause of teenage eye-rolls. (life of a teenage mum)

Until one day she asked, "Aaargh!!! how can I make sure they don't get dirty!!!?! "

Ah! FINALLY....my 60 seconds of extempore begins here & now!!

This is what I told her - Is your being extra cautious preventing it from becoming dirty? NO.

Wouldn't it be better if you just let them go through their journey as they are meant to be —getting dirty where they are meant to be? On their journey, they will leave impressions of their sole on surfaces and also gather dust, dirt, and stuff! because that's the 'purpose & the journey' of the shoe and its sole.

While that's something you caaan't control, What you can do is, Clean them : end of the day, once a week, a month ..whatever suits

Just don't let the cleaning become such a burden that you stop enjoying the shoes altogether.

Not sure if she got the point - shall update when she wears them next ;)

But then, later when I was feeling proud about what I told her, it hit me that....

The SOUL and the SOLE are similar that way! No wonder they are homophones!

Much like the sole of a shoe, our soul journeys through life, leaving impressions on others and gathering its own dust which are emotions, experiences, and connections with people we meet and situations we face.

You can't shield your soul from every hurtful comment or messy situation. The point is to let your soul do what it's meant to! Feel, connect, and live fully. And when it gets a little too heavy, Pause, clean it up, and decide what's worth keeping.

Because just like those Sunshine Shoes, every soul leaves traces of its journey on others. So, hop, jump, and dance your way through life! Dusty or not.

So.....here's to the journeys of SOLES and SOULS—walking, running, skipping, stumbling, and sometimes just standing still.

Because at the end of the day, it's not about spotless soles or untarnished souls. It's about the stories they carry, the lives they touch, and the way they shine. Irrespective of the dust and dirt!!

Beautiful souls recognize beautiful souls. Keep being genuine!

www.ingramcontent.com/pod-product-compliance
Lightning Source LLC
Chambersburg PA
CBHW022012150726
47990CB00002B/626